The
Energies of
2025

The Energies of 2025

A Weekly Guide to the
Dynamic Forces
Shaping Your Year Ahead

Channeled by
Theresa Walstra

Published by Yes!Press
an imprint of Quickfox Publishing
www.quickfox.co.za

The Energies of 2025: A Weekly Guide to the Dynamic Forces Shaping Your Year Ahead

First edition 2024

Copyright ©2024 Theresa Walstra

All rights reserved

All rights reserved. No part of this book may be reprinted, reproduced or utilised in any form electronic, mechanical, or other means, now known or hereafter invented, including photocopying, and recording, or in any information storage or retrieval system, without permission in writing from the author: theresa@theresawalstra.com

CONTENTS

Foreword 7
Introduction 9
The general energy of 2025 19
Week-by-week energy keywords 25
January 29
February 35
March 41
April 45
May 51
June 55
July 61
August 67
September 73
October 79
November 85
December 91
Conclusion 95

FOREWORD

The information in this book was provided by my senior Spirit Guide, Cynthia, who speaks on behalf of the collective of Guides that work with me to offer insights and guidance. This material was channeled in early November 2024.

In this book, Cynthia provides an overview of the energetic themes you can expect in the year ahead, along with a week-by-week breakdown of what to anticipate. These themes also serve as the foundation for the weekly *Energy of the Week* updates. Each update includes a 5-minute channeled guided meditation designed to help you align with and make the most of that week's energies. Details on how to sign up for these updates are provided below and at the end of this book.

FOREWORD

It's helpful to remember that, from Cynthia's perspective, energies are neither inherently good nor bad. While our limited perspective may interpret them differently, all energies ultimately support our growth and highest good.

The goal of this book is to give you a head start and help you feel more prepared for the year's shifting energies. My hope is that you'll be able to work with these energies constructively to enhance your life and facilitate any changes you may need to make.

To support your journey, I've included blank *Reflections* pages for you to jot down your own insights about the energies of each month and how they've manifested in your life. Journaling in this way can deepen your understanding and lead to further personal insights.

For more in-depth guidance and to subscribe to the *Energy of the Week* updates, email Theresa:

theresa@theresawalstra.com

Theresa Walstra

INTRODUCTION

Let's start with a prayer, and then the guides will come through.

Great Spirit, we ask for your protection as we join the world of spirit. We ask that you help us to open our minds, our hearts, and our lives so that we can hear and understand the important information that is relevant to each of us. We ask that you bless what we are doing here.

Cynthia begins ...

So we greet you once again, beloved friends, and as we draw toward you at this time, we bring with us many from the spirit world who come to guide you, care for you, and protect you.

Let us begin by explaining energies.

Energy in your world, in our world, and in every world that exists... is *everything*. There is nothing that exists, in any form, without energy.

INTRODUCTION

We would say that the spirit world is perhaps the largest of all worlds known to us, and in the spirit world, *everything* is energy—nothing is physical. So, when a transition takes place from your world to ours, it occurs in the form of energy.

But energy is also used in your world. As your world—the material world you call the Earth plane—evolves, growing more and more, the acknowledgment of energy becomes greater. While you rely on your five senses—the senses of taste, touch, sight, hearing, and smell—there is also the emotional sense of yourself, and this too is connected with energy.

On some level, you all recognise energy. For some, the recognition of energy is stronger than for others. Everything you do, every thought you have, and every sensation you experience is connected with energy.

It is important to understand that energy is paramount to understanding your life as you live it in your human condition and the life of spirit as it will be lived when you transition. Energetically, not all of who you are as spirit (your spirit-self)

INTRODUCTION

can incarnate into the earthly plane. Much more of your spirit-self remains in the spirit world than is incarnated in any physical form. Only a small part of your spirit incarnates.

Working with energy offers clues about how best to handle the circumstances of your life. Those of you who follow the *Energy of the Week* recordings (in which you are given an understanding of the energy available each week, along with a five-minute talk and a five-minute meditation) will have noticed that, no matter what your life circumstances may be, the weekly energy can be applied to those circumstances—to whatever is happening within and around you. This is because energy is constantly affecting you. By following the energy of the week, you will see just how much life and energy can shift from one moment to the next.

Energy is expansive. Energy does not arrive or depart at an exact moment. Energies overlap and intertwine; they work together and against each other. While we speak of the energy of the week, some energies may become dominant during a particular week and last for six, eight, or

INTRODUCTION

even 12 weeks or longer. Other energies may be shorter-lived and less dominant.

Whatever energy becomes available in your world, it is energy sent into your world and designed specifically to support your growth, the growth of the world, and the growth of everyone incarnated in the earthly plane.

Energy has an effect beyond what you would call your solar system. There is always an interaction of energetic attachments. Energy in your world affects other worlds, and energy in other worlds affects yours.

The energy available to you connects you with more than just the physical world. You can use energy to connect with the spirit world, and you can use it to connect with others in your world. Energetic links are immensely powerful, though they are often unrecognised. For example, if you wish to connect with someone who is not in your geographical location, you can use energy to create that connection. Similarly, you can use energy to connect with someone in the spirit world who has transitioned.

INTRODUCTION

Energy is also increasingly used in new ways in your world. Advances in technology are based on energy, which has always served as a portal through which you can move as a "substance." Energy can enhance or diminish you—it can benefit you if you connect with it positively or harm you if you engage with it negatively.

What is fascinating is that those born into your world have access to energy on a far greater level than is acknowledged. However, as they grow and are influenced by conditioning, their attachment to energy often diminishes. As their attachment wanes, they become less powerful.

You must recognise that energy is everything. There is nothing that does not work with energy. Energy is vital to understanding your circumstances, yourself, and life itself.

Consider astrology: its foundation lies in energy and the interactions between planets through their alignments. Certain alignments create specific energies, which are relevant because they originate in a vast universe far beyond your current understanding. These energies are influenced by

INTRODUCTION

planets, stars, and everything within the universe. Your perception of existence is limited when compared with the actual vastness of life and energy.

Take the energy of healing: everyone in your world has access to healing energy. None of you would ever think healing energy is finite or needs to be rationed. You innately understand that healing energy is infinite.

All energy is infinite, yet as it channels through pathways into your world, it impacts planets and other energetic sources. In this way, energy has an immense effect on life. Never underestimate energy.

How often do you wake up feeling perfect one day and completely different the next, even though nothing has outwardly changed? This is because energy surrounds and fills you, and its fluctuations are inevitable.

You may also notice how easy it is to pick up on the energy of others. For instance, being in an environment filled with hopelessness or negativity can pull you into that energy, even

INTRODUCTION

if you resist it. Similarly, you might feel the discontent or negativity of others shaping your thoughts and emotions.

Whatever energy you draw into yourself is the energy you exude. While some energetic influences are beyond your control, there are energies you can—and should—seek to manage.

The energies that enter your world are not inherently "bad," though they may have a negative effect depending on how you engage with them. Every energy, no matter how difficult it may seem, can be used to enhance your life if you work with it consciously.

As you move through life, rather than asking, "What happened?" consider, "Which energy is impacting me, and how can I best work with it?" Working with your guides or through meditation, you can use energy—whether it appears positive or negative—to your advantage, as long as you acknowledge and accept it.

Now, we present a list of weekly energies for 2025. We want to say that in giving you this overview, we have chosen to call it "Energy of the Week"

INTRODUCTION

simply because it makes it easier for us to provide you with information and meditations that you can apply to your lives for the most *dominant* energy at any given time.

The weeks and the corresponding energies are first summarised, and a more detailed description of each is provided further on in the book.

Now, as we look at the year 2025, you are once again looking at what may well be a challenging year. There will be a dominant energy of what we would call **self-centeredness**.

This energy will apply in many different ways, as you will see when we go through the calendar week by week. However, like everything else, energy can be used to your benefit or against you. What determines that is the choices you make.

So, no matter the circumstances, if you are aware of the dominant energy, you can use it to your benefit—no matter what is happening in your life, around you, or in the lives of others.

INTRODUCTION

We would say to you: *it remains up to you to make the best possible choices as you move through the year that lies ahead.*

Now, let us move into the 2025 energy overview, and the week-by-week forecast.

THE GENERAL ENERGY OF 2025

The most dominant energies in your world for 2025 revolve around control and, consequently, manipulation. This makes 2025 a significant year, offering opportunities for growth and learning both for those who tend to control and those who allow themselves to be controlled.

Control manifests in many aspects of life. It's worth reflecting on how often you, as an individual, may try to control life itself—overriding what the universe is providing for you. Sometimes, a person wants something so desperately that they hold their life in a "death grip," refusing to allow flow and feeling compelled to control every single aspect of their lives. This effort to "force" life to conform to their demands or dreams creates imbalance, often delaying or derailing progress toward the very goals they long for.

Control also becomes apparent when individuals or groups force others to agree with them. At every level—whether individuals, organizations, or governments—you will see intense manipulation as they attempt to impose their choices on others.

This year will bring a unique perspective on control, particularly as it relates to the legacy of the "pandemic." Many individuals and groups may choose not to allow the same type of control to happen again. However, the tendency to accept control in different forms will remain. For example, some individuals will continue to trust those in power to make decisions for them, as long as the control does not mirror previous patterns.

Skilled manipulators—whether individuals or groups—will adapt their methods, speaking in ways that reduce the likelihood of their control being rejected. On a larger scale, control will be enforced through laws. You will likely see a marked increase in new laws worldwide, often only partially explained to ensure they are accepted, paving the way for control to be imposed.

THE GENERAL ENERGY OF 2025

For those who often allow or even expect to be controlled, this year will provide continuous opportunities to break free from those patterns.

On a personal level, especially within relationships, many people will face abuse but struggle to step away from it. The year 2025 is all about choices. Each individual will have the opportunity to break old patterns, adopt new behaviors, and, in many ways, re-create themselves.

Words, actions, and thoughts can be examined through the lens of self-analysis, with particular attention to the dominant energy of control. Consider asking yourself these questions throughout 2025:

- Am I trying too hard to control the outcome?
- Is the universe providing me with tools that I'm overriding in my need to control?
- Am I trying too hard to manipulate the choices of others?
- Am I making a choice because I truly want to, or because someone else wants me to?
- Am I living in the moment with anxiety or with peace?

- Am I overlooking an unexpected opportunity the universe is providing because I believe there is only one pathway?
- Am I allowing the potential energies of change to flow into my life?
- Am I in harmony with the constant shifts of life and love?

Remember, 2025 is simply the next year in your journey. You will experience far less stress, anxiety, and tension if you recognize how much help is available to you from the spirit world.

Your Spirit Guides are highly trained, skilled, and knowledgeable. Their sole purpose is to guide you through the life you are living. If you could release your need to control every outcome and plan for every eventuality, and instead simply listen and allow, you would find your guides are always waiting for your request for help.

You are loved beyond measure. You are fully understood. Your guides and the universe are providing exactly what you need to ensure your progress—right now!

THE GENERAL ENERGY OF 2025

Reflections

THE GENERAL ENERGY OF 2025

Reflections

WEEK-BY-WEEK ENERGY KEYWORDS

January
5 January: Jealousy
12 January: Charm
19 January: Patience
26 January: Logic

February
2 February: Wisdom
9 February: Variability
16 February: Consequence
23 February: Desire

March
2 March: Opportunity
9 March: Delight
16 March: Favor
23 March: Impossibility
30 March: Courage

April

6 April: Control
13 April: Demand
20 April: Revenge
27 April: Abundance

May

4 May: Regret
11 May: Relief
18 May: Expansion
25 May: Introspection

June

1 June: Love
8 June: Awareness
15 June: Clarity
22 June: Success
29 June: Generosity

July

6 July: Forcefulness
13 July: Manipulation
20 July: Release
27 July: Betrayal

August

3 August: Callousness
10 August: Vigilance
17 August: Temperance
24 August: Victimisation
31 August: Loneliness

September

7 September: Migration
14 September: Planning
21 September: Inattention
28 September: Anxiety

October

5 October: Control
12 October: Power
19 October: Alertness
26 October: Stealth

November

2 November: Chaos
9 November: Stability
16 November: Strength
23 November: Progress
30 November: Peace

December

7 December: Trust
14 December: Acceptance
21 December: Relaxation
28 December: Dreams

JANUARY

5 January: Jealousy
12 January: Charm
19 January: Patience
26 January: Logic

January starts with the energy of **jealousy**. This has an increased effect because, toward the end of December 2024, you are looking at circumstances where you may be making progress. Those of you who have the energy of peace and the power of peace that you use within your life will definitely be making progress. The December 2024 energies of release, relaxation, and flow lead to you (and others—even if they are unaware of the energies) becoming successful. Success, in the eyes of others, has the effect of making others jealous, and that's the dominant energy as the year begins—an energy of jealousy. You will find that peace and success increase the potential for all sorts of jealousies.

The second week of January brings in an energy of **charm**, so you are likely to be charmed by circumstances, and you are likely to find yourself charming others. It's a delicate energy, but it can be very effective. We recommend that you keep this in mind when the energy of jealousy is present, as these two overlap to a certain extent. As charm becomes more dominant, you will have the energy of charm to persuade others and perhaps dampen the jealousy energy.

Patience follows in the third week of January. The energy of patience won't last very long; in your world, patience seldom lasts for any significant amount of time. However, as it becomes dominant, you can use it to teach yourself to adjust to patience. If you have difficulty being patient, you need to use this energy during the third week of January to teach yourself to be more patient with yourself and with others, but mainly with yourself. If you are an impatient person, you can be certain that you are far more impatient with yourself than with others. What is seen by others is often just a fraction of the impatience you apply to your own life. This is a very good skill to learn in the third week of January and to carry through the rest of your life.

The fourth week of January provides an energy of **logic**. This energy is valuable but can also be challenging if you are an overthinker. If you have a tendency to overthink, you may find difficulties arising. It's important to work carefully with this energy.

JANUARY

Reflections

JANUARY

Reflections

JANUARY

Reflections

FEBRUARY

2 February: Wisdom
9 February: Variability
16 February: Consequence
23 February: Desire

The first week of February builds on the energy of logic by providing **wisdom**. We would say that knowledge and experience can be translated into wisdom. This energy allows you to apply the logic and thinking from the previous week in the best possible way. Wisdom, of course, exists at different levels. There are many who may not seem wise to you but who are wise by their own measure. This energy allows everyone the opportunity to increase their wisdom—to apply their knowledge and experience to become wiser. Wisdom is about integrating experience and logic into who you are, allowing you to shift your perception of yourself and other aspects of life.

The second week of February brings an interesting energy of **variability**, meaning changeability. This is a time where everything changes. There is movement; things will not be as you expect them to be. You yourself may not be as you expect, and others may be surprised by your words, thoughts, or actions. You will appear variable instead of static—constantly changing. Variability can be both positive and negative, affecting your personality, others' personalities, and expectations. If you are seeking to trust someone, this is not the week to test that trust. First, understand that the variability of nature is dominant, and it will prevail no matter what.

The third week of February introduces the energy of **consequence**. It's almost as though the actions, thoughts, and choices you've made over the last two to three years (or longer) come to fruition. If you've made unwise choices in the past, their consequences may now surface—whether as actual events, thoughts, or emotional realisations. This could be a challenging week for many.

FEBRUARY

The final week of February brings the energy of **desire**. Following the energy of consequence—where you've reflected on the outcomes of your choices and noticed that some are not to your liking—you may begin to desire changes in your life and lifestyle. This energy of desire can guide you towards new goals; think of it as a reset for your navigational direction in life.

FEBRUARY

Reflections

FEBRUARY

Reflections

FEBRUARY

Reflections

MARCH

2 March: Opportunity
9 March: Delight
16 March: Favor
23 March: Impossibility
30 March: Courage

The energy of desire from February links closely to the energy of **opportunity** in March. The universe offers a chance to pursue what you desire, presenting opportunities to move toward what you wish to achieve. It is a beautiful week. However, those with self-centered intentions may use this opportunity to selfishly pursue their own goals, sometimes at the expense of others.

The second week of March brings the energy of **delight**, which allows you to notice and appreciate what brings you joy. Large or small, circumstances around you will provide opportunities to delight in life itself—a truly beautiful energy.

The third week of March carries the energy of **favor**. This energy can be a double-edged sword. You may find yourself giving favors and prioritizing others over yourself. Those who are self-centered may take advantage of this generosity. While it can be a positive energy, it is important to recognize and manage its potential negative effects.

The fourth week of March brings the energy of **impossibility**. This energy provides a chance to make what seems impossible achievable. It's as though the universe challenges you to stretch beyond your perceived limits.

The final week of March introduces the energy of **courage**, beautifully placed after opportunity, delight, favor, and impossibility. This energy empowers you to make choices you might not have made before. It is a strong, transformative energy that could make March a powerful month if you align with its potential.

MARCH

Reflections

MARCH

Reflections

APRIL

6 April: Control
13 April: Demand
20 April: Revenge
27 April: Abundance

In April, you will encounter head-on the energy that dominates the entirety of 2025—the energy of **control**. Control means that others will seek to dominate. You will see this need to control in governments, institutions, and organisations, which may create dominating power structures to control the lives of others. You may see new laws or rules come into effect, further restricting individuals or even countries. This dominant energy is one you need to use to your benefit to find peace, regardless of circumstances. You will need to find ways to create freedom for yourself, even in situations where control is imposed. You may also feel the urge to control circumstances or people around you, but this is a time to practise discipline and resist that need. This energy, by and large, is not a positive one, but it can teach important lessons.

In the second week of April, the energy shifts to **demand**. Demands will be made on people, groups, and circumstances—often demands that cannot be met. You may witness acts of cruelty during this time. The energies of April are designed to trigger individuals and groups with tendencies towards unkindness or cruelty, while simultaneously creating opportunities for others to respond with kindness and compassion. One energy triggers a shadow response, while others bring light and growth through kindness. Remember, these are the dominant energies available at this time. Many will perceive the events as "evil" coming to power in the world. However, we remind you that in the truest sense, evil does not exist—only choices do.

The third week of April brings the energy of **revenge**. This energy may emerge as those who have been dominated start to push back, creating further conflict, turmoil, and chaos.

At the same time, acts of kindness in response to this energy will provide balance and an opportunity for growth. The energies of control, demand, and revenge in the first three weeks of April reflect the essence of self-centeredness, which dominates much of 2025. You are tasked with finding peace amidst these energies, as peace remains the greatest power available to you. When you operate from peace, you operate from a position of strength and clarity.

The fourth week of April introduces the energy of **abundance**. This energy is universal and provides abundance for everyone. However, those who have engaged in unkindness and control may attract an abundance of these same energies into their lives. To make the best use of this energy, link it to peace and opportunity. By doing so, you can bring greater abundance into your life—whether it is financial, emotional, or spiritual—than you have experienced before.

Reflections

APRIL

Reflections

APRIL

Reflections

MAY

4 May: Regret
11 May: Relief
18 May: Expansion
25 May: Introspection

May begins with the energy of **regret**. This energy calls on you to acknowledge the mistakes or missteps you perceive in your past. It is not about going back to fix these mistakes but about recognising them and releasing the guilt associated with them. Regret surfaces to help you understand and let go of burdens you may have been carrying unconsciously.

In the second week, the energy shifts to **relief**. If you have used the energy of regret constructively, the energy of relief will be immense. It offers a profound sense of freedom, as you let go of guilt and regret and embrace self-acceptance and understanding. This energy also encourages forgiveness of yourself, creating space for emotional liberation.

The third week of May brings the energy of **expansion**. This beautiful energy allows you to feel more open and free, no longer constrained by self-imposed boundaries. It encourages you to embrace who you truly are and to step into a more expansive and liberated version of yourself.

The fourth week of May introduces **introspection**. This energy invites you to turn inward, reflecting on all the energies you have experienced throughout the month. It is a time for self-conversation and deep internal reflection. This energy may make external communication more challenging, as your focus shifts inward. Use this time to connect with yourself and gain greater clarity about your life.

Reflections

MAY

Reflections

JUNE

1 June: Love
8 June: Awareness
15 June: Clarity
22 June: Success
29 June: Generosity

The month of June begins with the energy of **love**. This energy helps you understand the lessons you have learned from previous months and offers an opportunity for self-love. By embracing love for yourself, you can reflect love outwardly into the world, creating harmonious relationships and connections. This energy is transformative and can significantly impact your life. Even those who start from a place of lacking love will experience its effects, although it may not be immediately apparent.

The second week brings the energy of **awareness**. Having turned inward during May and embraced love in the first week of June, you now begin to observe the external world with fresh eyes. Awareness enables you to see how the world affects you and how you affect the world, setting the stage for deeper communication and connection.

The third week offers **clarity**. Awareness leads to clear, focused thoughts and decisions. This energy helps you see your life with greater understanding, though it may still be tinged with lingering emotions from past weeks. Use this clarity to make thoughtful, informed choices.

The fourth week introduces the energy of **success**. This energy allows you to see the results of your hard work and perseverance. For some, success may align with positive intentions, while for others, it may stem from self-serving or harmful actions. This energy is universal and reflects the choices and intentions of each individual.

JUNE

The final week of June brings **generosity**. This energy asks you to consider how you give to others and to yourself. Generosity, when paired with awareness, clarity, and love, becomes a balanced and thoughtful act. Use this energy to reflect on the ways in which you offer support and care, ensuring it is sustainable and rooted in genuine compassion.

JUNE

Reflections

JUNE

Reflections

Reflections

JULY

6 July: Forcefulness
13 July: Manipulation
20 July: Release
27 July: Betrayal

As we move into July, the energies reflect themes of control and self-centeredness seen throughout 2025.

The first week introduces the energy of **forcefulness**. People may attempt to force their opinions, beliefs, or choices onto others. It is important to recognise that this energy also applies to you. You may feel strong opinions about how others should act or think, and this is a reminder to step back. This energy offers you the opportunity to learn not to impose your will or views on others.

The second week of July brings the energy of **manipulation**. This energy, while less overt than forcefulness, still reflects a form of control. It is subtler and more covert but can be equally impactful. You can, however, use the energies of forcefulness and manipulation positively by applying them with love, kindness, and peace. In this way, these challenging energies can become tools for positive transformation, rather than harm.

The third week of July introduces the energy of **release**. This is a beautiful energy, as it allows those who have been held captive—physically, emotionally, or metaphorically—by the forcefulness or manipulation of others to find a sense of freedom. This energy may not always mean physical liberation, but it provides an emotional and mental release, bringing peace and a sense of freedom. It is a valuable energy that can be used at many levels of life.

JULY

The final week of July brings the energy of **betrayal**. This energy, a remnant of 2024, resurfaces. If you have been learning from the experiences of betrayal in the previous year, you will be better equipped to handle its effects now. It encourages you to recognise, understand, and avoid the pitfalls of betrayal, using the lessons learned to navigate this challenging energy.

Reflections

JULY

Reflections

JULY

Reflections

AUGUST

3 August: Callousness
10 August: Vigilance
17 August: Temperance
24 August: Victimisation
31 August: Loneliness

August begins with the energy of **callousness**. This energy reflects the recurring themes of self-centeredness, control, and unkindness. Callousness manifests as a disregard for the feelings of others and a lack of empathy. Even if you are a kind and compassionate person, you will be exposed to this energy. By recognising its presence, you can minimise its impact on your life and the lives of others.

The second week of August brings the energy of **vigilance**. This energy acts as a shield, allowing individuals to protect themselves from the unkindness and cruelty that may surround them.

Vigilance provides an opportunity to safeguard your heart and life, offering protection during challenging times.

The third week introduces the energy of **temperance**. This energy seeks to balance and moderate extremes. It can soften the severity of unkindness and cruelty in the world, while at a personal level, it encourages you to moderate behaviours, habits, or thoughts that may not serve you well. It is an opportunity to find equilibrium and ease.

The fourth week of August brings the energy of **victimisation**. While everyone has experienced victimisation at some point, this energy intensifies that sense. It is especially challenging for those who tend to dwell on feelings of being wronged. This week, pay close attention to your inner dialogue. Avoid falling into the "poor me" mindset and remember that your choices shape your experiences. The energy of victimisation offers a lesson: to avoid letting this energy take hold too deeply and to rise above it.

AUGUST

The final week of August introduces the energy of **loneliness**. This energy encourages self-observation. Even if you are not alone, you may feel a sense of isolation. You might find yourself wishing for different circumstances or connections. This energy highlights areas of longing or dissatisfaction, offering a chance to identify what is missing in your life and to address those needs. While it may feel harsh, it is a valuable opportunity for growth and understanding.

AUGUST

Reflections

AUGUST

Reflections

AUGUST

Reflections

SEPTEMBER

7 September: Migration
14 September: Planning
21 September: Inattention
28 September: Anxiety

As you move into September, you encounter some intriguing energies.

The first week brings the energy of **migration**. This may manifest as a desire to move or relocate, though it doesn't always mean a physical move. It could reflect a longing to change aspects of your life, inspired by the sense of emptiness or dissatisfaction highlighted in August. This energy encourages you to explore what draws you to a particular place or change, asking what it reveals about your deeper desires and needs.

The second week introduces the energy of **planning**. Building on the reflections of migration, this energy helps you consider how to bring about the changes you desire. It offers an opportunity to thoughtfully map out steps to create a better, more fulfilling life for yourself and those you care about.

The third week of September brings the energy of **inattention**. This energy creates distraction and a lack of focus. Even those who are typically detail-oriented may find themselves inattentive, asking others to repeat things or missing important details. This energy also reflects a deeper connection with the higher self, which prioritises spiritual matters over physical concerns. While it may feel frustrating, it is an invitation to connect with your higher self and gain a broader perspective on life.

The final week introduces the energy of **anxiety**. This energy, while uncomfortable, serves an important purpose. Anxiety creates a sense of discontent, prompting you to make necessary changes. It asks, "What can I do now?" and pushes you to take action towards improvement. When viewed as a gift, this energy can be transformative, driving progress and growth.

SEPTEMBER

Reflections

Reflections

SEPTEMBER

Reflections

OCTOBER

5 October: Control
12 October: Power
19 October: Alertness
26 October: Stealth

October begins with a return of the energy of **control**. This energy, as seen earlier in the year, can manifest in various ways, from subtle to overt. You may witness control being exerted by individuals, groups, or governments, creating walls between people, communities, or even nations. It is a time when the desire to dominate resurfaces, often resulting in unpleasant consequences. However, this energy also provides an opportunity for you to observe and learn from it, enabling you to find ways to remain centred and maintain inner peace amidst external pressures.

The second week brings the energy of **power**. Power, like control, can be used in two very distinct ways: it can benefit yourself and others, or it can be wielded selfishly to the detriment of others. For you, this energy asks that you align it with peace, remembering that the greatest power comes from operating in harmony and kindness. This week challenges you to use power positively and constructively, while many others may use it self-centeredly, causing harm and imbalance.

The third week introduces the energy of **alertness**. This energy heightens awareness and provides a sense of readiness. It acts as a protective force, encouraging individuals to remain vigilant in the face of potential manipulation or control. For you, it can be an excellent tool to enhance mental clarity, helping you make informed and conscious choices.

The final week of October brings the energy of **stealth**. This energy often relates to hidden actions and plans. While stealth can be used positively—for thoughtful preparation or careful

OCTOBER

strategy—it is more commonly associated with secrecy and covert intentions. During this time, you may notice unseen forces at play, where individuals or groups position themselves to gain power or control. By tapping into your intuition, you can perceive what is not immediately visible and navigate this energy with wisdom.

Reflections

OCTOBER

Reflections

OCTOBER

Reflections

NOVEMBER

2 November: Chaos
9 November: Stability
16 November: Strength
23 November: Progress
30 November: Peace

November begins with the energy of **chaos**. Following the energy of stealth from October, chaos comes as a disruptor, preventing any one group or individual from gaining excessive power or control. While this energy can feel unsettling, it also serves a protective purpose, breaking apart harmful systems and creating space for renewal.

The second week introduces the energy of **stability**. Interestingly, stability is not automatically granted—it is an energy you must choose and anchor into your life. In a time of chaos, the ability to create stability becomes a powerful tool. By choosing to ground yourself, you can find a sense of calm and balance that supports your well-being.

The third week brings the energy of **strength**. Strength, like power, can be used in positive or negative ways. For you, it offers the chance to reinforce the stability you've built, deepening your resilience and resolve. It encourages you to align with inner strength to face challenges with confidence and clarity.

The fourth week introduces the energy of **progress**. Building on stability and strength, this energy helps you take steps forward in your life. It is an opportunity to harness all the lessons and growth from the year to create meaningful movement towards your goals.

The final week of November offers the energy of **peace**. As with stability, peace is a choice. You have the opportunity to align yourself with this energy, using it to counteract the chaos and challenges of the year.

NOVEMBER

Peace, when chosen, becomes a powerful foundation for the future and a source of immense strength and clarity.

NOVEMBER

Reflections

NOVEMBER

Reflections

Reflections

DECEMBER

7 December: Trust
14 December: Acceptance
21 December: Relaxation
28 December: Dreams

December begins with the energy of **trust**. This energy helps you discern who and what you can trust. It also encourages you to trust yourself, building confidence in your choices and instincts. It is a beautiful energy that fosters deeper connections with yourself and others.

The second week brings the energy of **acceptance**. This energy allows you to let go of resistance and embrace what is. When paired with trust, it creates a sense of contentment and peace, enabling you to move forward with clarity and ease. Acceptance does not mean surrendering to harmful control or dominance but rather finding balance and understanding in the circumstances of your life.

DECEMBER

The third week introduces the energy of **relaxation**. After the intensity of the year, this energy offers a chance to breathe and rest. By using the energies of trust and acceptance, you can fully embrace this period of relaxation, allowing yourself to recharge and prepare for what lies ahead.

The final week of December brings the energy of **dreams**. This energy invites you to explore both waking dreams and those experienced during sleep. It provides an opportunity to envision what your life can become, to reconnect with your aspirations, and to imagine new possibilities. As the year comes to a close, this energy serves as a perfect culmination, offering hope and inspiration for the future.

DECEMBER

Reflections

DECEMBER

Reflections

CONCLUSION

This concludes the energy overview for 2025.

We hope we have provided you with some interesting insights and valuable information. We encourage you to make use of this guidance to harness the prevailing energies and empower your life.

Each energy offers an opportunity for growth and transformation. By remaining mindful and intentional, you can navigate these energies to your greatest benefit.

In addition to this information, we suggest joining the *Energy of the Week* podcast. Each week, you can listen to the five-minute talk and the five-minute meditation to gain deeper insights into the weekly energies and learn how to apply them to your life.

CONCLUSION

Listening to the guided meditations—all of which are channeled by Cynthia through the mediumship of Theresa Walstra—will fully activate these energies and help you navigate them with greater ease and grace.

If you would like to sign up for the weekly *Energy of the Week* talks and meditations for 2025, please email:

theresa@theresawalstra.com

We leave you in the care of your own Spirit Guides and those who love you from the spirit world.

We send you our great and unconditional love.

About Theresa and her Guides

Although trained and experienced as an analytical chemist, Theresa Walstra comes from a long maternal lineage of gifted clairvoyants. She began her journey as a clairvoyant in the 1990s and started channeling her Spirit Guides in 1997.

Theresa, in collaboration with her Guides, has worked with clients worldwide, offering advice, healing, and guidance in a variety of situations.

She is the author of *The Mechanics of Mediumship* and co-author of *Beloved Friend* and *A Spiritual Toolkit for Dealing with Change*. Her latest book, *The Energies of 2025*, is based on a live channeling session conducted in late 2024.

In addition to writing, Theresa facilitates online courses and workshops, has appeared on radio and online media, and continues to provide consultations to clients globally.

Connect with Theresa on Facebook or through email: theresa@theresawalstra.com

www.ingramcontent.com/pod-product-compliance
Lightning Source LLC
Chambersburg PA
CBHW030455010526
44118CB00011B/942